How do things
Grow?

Library of Congress Cataloging-in-Publication Data

Althea.
    How do things grow? / by Althea; illustrated by Julie
Douglas.
        p.   cm.
    Summary: Discusses how plants and animals gain energy, change, and
grow through the course of their existence.
    ISBN 0-8167-2118-1 (lib. bdg.)   ISBN 0-8167-2119-X (pbk.)
    1. Growth—Juvenile literature.   2. Human growth—Juvenile
literature.   [1. Growth.]   I. Douglas, Julie, ill.   II. Title.
QH511.A48   1991
574.3'1—dc20   90-10923

Published by Troll Associates, Mahwah, New Jersey 07430

Copyright © 1991 by Eagle Books Limited

Printed in the U.S.A.

10 9 8 7 6 5 4 3 2 1

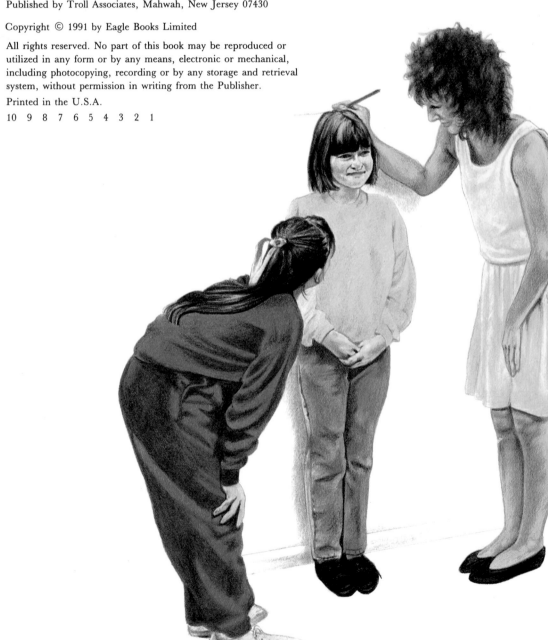

How do things Grow?

Written by
Althea

Illustrated by
Julie Douglas

Troll Associates

People, animals, and plants
need food and water
to make them grow.
Plants also need light.
Their green leaves use energy
directly from the sun
to make their food.

Some animals eat plants to
get their energy.
Others eat animals
which have eaten plants.
Energy, which comes from sunlight,
is stored in the food we eat.

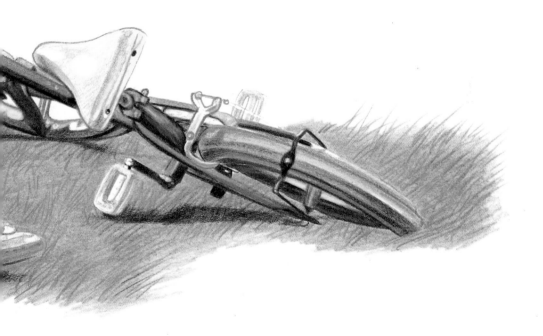

Crack the shell of an unroasted peanut
and plant it in wet soil.
After a few days the root
will start to grow down,
and a week later green leaves
will grow upward.

Plants grow from seeds.
Food is stored in the seeds.
To start growing, seeds must
be warm and wet.

You need food and water
to give you energy and
to make you grow.
Parts of you grow quickly
like your hair and nails.
When did you last
have your hair cut?
How often do your nails
need cutting?
The rest of your body
grows more slowly.

Proteins, vitamins, and minerals
in food make us grow new skin cells
all the time.
If you fall and cut yourself,
new skin will grow back.

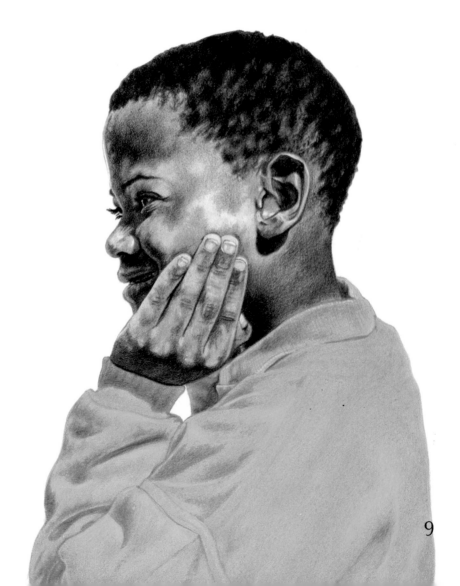

As you grow bigger, your bones
and skin grow too.
You get taller and you weigh more.
You grow too big for your clothes,
and you need to get new ones.

Some animals grow a new skin.
As snakes grow bigger, their skin
becomes too tight and splits.
The snake wriggles out, and shiny
new skin is ready underneath.

Some animals live inside shells
which protect their soft bodies.
Snails live in shells which
grow bigger with them.
But hermit crabs do not
grow their own shells.
When a hermit crab grows
too big for its shell, it has to find
another, bigger one to move into.

Kittens, puppies, and many other animals
lose their first teeth like us.
Some animals wear their teeth
down by gnawing their food.
Rabbits and rats have some teeth
which keep on growing all their lives.
Pet rabbits need a gnawing block
to stop their teeth from growing
too long.

We have two sets of teeth.
When your first teeth fall out,
the new ones are already pushing
their way through your gums.

Our teeth stop growing when
the top and bottom rows
reach the right size to bite
together to chew our food.

Puppies with large paws
usually grow to be big dogs.
But some people with large
hands and feet are not very tall.

Trace your hand so you can
check to see when it grows bigger.
After six months, put the same hand
on the drawing and trace it
with a different color.
You can see if it has grown.

You know when your feet grow
because your shoes get too tight.
You know when your legs grow
because your jeans become too short.

By the time you were two years old,
you were about half your adult height.
Can you remember when you couldn't
reach up to open the door or
turn on the light switch?
How high can you reach now?

Ask someone to measure your height.
Mark it on a measuring chart
or on the edge of a door.
Measure your mom or dad, too.

After six months, measure
your heights again.
You can see if you have grown
since last time.
Have your parents stopped
growing upward?
Most people stop growing upward
before they are eighteen or so.

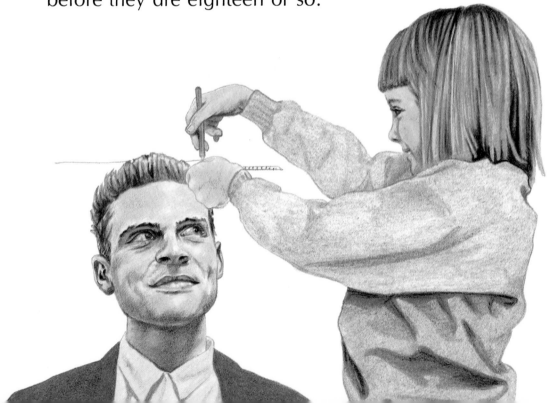

Not everything grows upward.
Some things grow outward.
Blow air into a balloon.
The rubber stretches and
it grows in size.

After a big meal, your stomach
is like the balloon!
Your stomach is filled with food.
Do your clothes feel tight
around your waist?
If you always eat too much,
you grow outward and need
new clothes.

People grow upward and
outward at different times.
You may have a friend
who is younger than you,
but who is taller than you!
When you are fully grown,
you might be taller than
your friend.

Most people and animals grow
to be like their parents.
Who do people say you look like –
your mom or your dad?

Plant some sunflower seeds.
They will grow taller than
you, and have flowers in
less than a year.

Trees grow from seeds,
but they will take many years
to grow taller than you.

Most baby animals look much the
same as their parents, only smaller.
But some animals change their
looks and their shape as they grow.

Tadpoles hatch from frogs' eggs.
They look like tiny fish.
They live in water, feeding first
on plants, then on tiny animals.
After a while, the tadpole
grows long back legs,
then front legs.
Soon its lungs grow and
it loses its tail.
The tiny frog is ready to
leave the water and hop away.

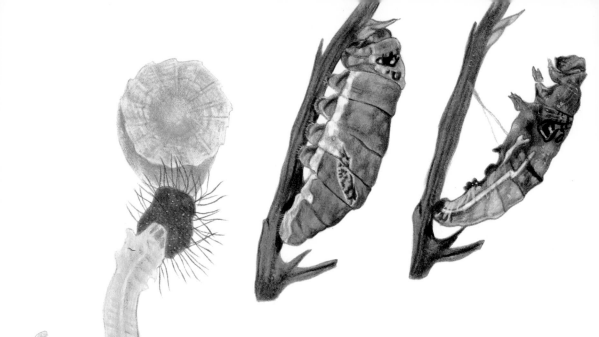

Butterflies and other insects
also change as they grow.
The female butterfly lays eggs.
Tiny caterpillars hatch from the
eggs and eat leaves.
They grow bigger and bigger.
They change their skins many times.
When a caterpillar is fully grown,
its skin splits for the last time,
and underneath there is a pupa.

The pupa shell hardens to
protect the caterpillar while
it grows wings and changes
into a butterfly.
When it is ready, the pupa
cracks open and a new and
beautiful butterfly crawls out.

Would you like to change
and grow wings like that?

Instead of growing wings, you
could learn to fly an airplane,
or to be a glider pilot.
Can you remember learning
to ride a bike?
You learn new things and understand
much more as you grow older.

People sometimes say you will be able
to do things when you are grown up.
They don't usually mean when you
are taller, but when you get older.

You are a grownup
when you have stopped
growing upward.

What do you want to do
when you grow up?